100 TRILLION GOOD BACTERIA LIVING ON THE HUMAN BODY

PAUL ROCKETT

W
FRANKLIN WATTS
LONDON•SYDNEY

First published in 2014 by Franklin Watts

Franklin Watts
338 Euston Road
London NW1 3BH

Franklin Watts Australia
Level 17/207 Kent Street
Sydney, NSW 2000

Editor: Rachel Cooke
Design and illustration: Mark Ruffle
www.rufflebrothers.com

Dewey number: 579.3'163
HB ISBN: 978 1 4451 2673 9
Library ebook: 978 1 4451 2679 1

Printed in China

Franklin Watts is a division of Hachette
Children's Books, an Hachette UK
company.
www.hachette.co.uk

Picture credits: Kitch Bain/Shutterstock: 10;
Istvan Csak/Shutterstock: 19; Dr Kari Lounatmaa/
Sciencephoto: 6; Tyler Olson/Shutterstock: 24;
rogelson/Shutterstock: 12; John Spellman/Retna/
Corbis: 9; Sprint/Corbis : 29; wikipedia commons:
4b; Pan Xunbin/Shutterstock: 4t, 14.

*Throughout the book you are given data relating
to various pieces of information covering
the topic. The numbers will most likely be an
estimation based on research made over a
period of time and in a particular area. Some
other research may reach a different set of data,
and all these figures may change with time as
new research and information is gathered. The
numbers provided within this book are believed
to be correct at the time of printing and have
been sourced from the following sites:*
acneacademy.org; americanscientist.org;
anatomy.org; archive.food.gov.uk; atsjournals.
org; babycentre.co.uk; bbc.co.uk; bicepbuilder.
com; biomedcentral.com; biotopics.co.uk; blf.org.
uk; blood.ygoy.com; cs.rpi.edu; dailymail.co.uk;
dermatology.about.com; disabled-world.com;
docstoc.com; drstandley.com; ehso.com; eoearth.
org; facts.randomhistory.com; fitnesstogether.com;
fitpregnancy.com; guinnessworldrecords.com;
heartscan.com; heartfoundation.org.au; highered.
mcgraw-hill.com; howstuffworks.com; kidsbiology.
com; kidshealth.org; kidskonnect.com; library.
thinkquest.org; livestrong.com; livingnaturally.
com; my.clevelandclinic.org; mybloodyourblood.
org; naturessunshine.com; news.bbc.co.uk;
news.harvard.edu; news.softpedia.com;
newworldencyclopedia.org; nhs.uk; nidcd.nih.
gov; nlm.nih.gov; oprah.com; pigeonbooks.
com; research.msu.edu; rnceus.com; science.
howstuffworks.com; sciencedaily.com; sciencekids.
co.nz; scientificamerican.com; sharecare.com;
spinalphysio.co.uk; statastic.com; statisticbrain.
com; thbexhibition.com; theyiau.org.

CONTENTS

COUNTING DOWN THE HUMAN BODY

The human body is made up of external and internal organs. The external organs are everything that you can see on your body, such as your skin, nose and ears. The internal organs are underneath your skin and include your heart, lungs and brain.

EXTERNAL ORGANS

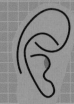

INTERNAL ORGANS

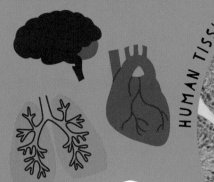

HUMAN TISSUE UNDER THE MICROSCOPE

Microscopes allow people to study the human body at a microscopic level – this means that the smallest living cells that make up your body can be viewed.

ANATOMY

The study of the human body in science is known as anatomy. The study of anatomy dates back to the ancient Egyptians around **1600 BCE**, when they showed an understanding of how the heart operates, possibly through the practice of human sacrifice.

To understand how the inside of the body works, the body had to be dissected. This means that the body was cut open to reveal what was inside.

Juan Valverde de Amusco, the Italian artist of this print from 1559, studied the human body by dissecting it. This print shows what lies under the skin.

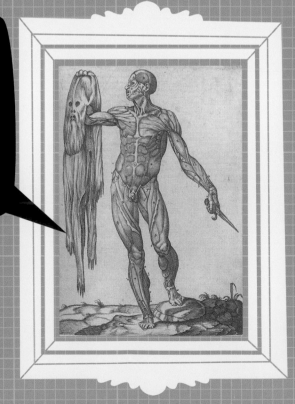

GROWING AND AGEING

Throughout your life your body continues to change. The body reaches full growth at around the age of **21 years**. Over the following years, your body still develops but it will not experience the same level of growth, for example you will not grow any taller. From this point on, the body starts an ageing process whereby the body is slower at repairing itself. Later in life the body will also begin to shrink. You will lose at least **1 cm** in height every decade after the age of **40**. By **80**, most men will be **5 cm** shorter and women **8 cm** shorter than they were in their **twenties**.

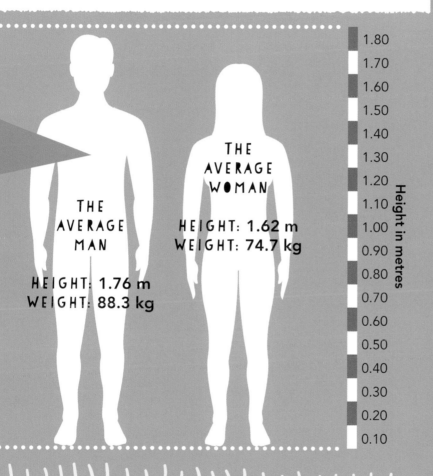

THE AVERAGE MAN

HEIGHT: 1.76 m
WEIGHT: 88.3 kg

THE AVERAGE WOMAN

HEIGHT: 1.62 m
WEIGHT: 74.7 kg

1.80
1.70
1.60
1.50
1.40
1.30
1.20
1.10
1.00
0.90
0.80
0.70
0.60
0.50
0.40
0.30
0.20
0.10

Height in metres

EVERYBODY'S BODY IS DIFFERENT

Bodies are different in shape, colour, the amount of hair they have or even in the number of fingers and toes they have. When talking about the human body, scientists will often refer to an average measurement to use as an example. This average will have been gained by studying many bodies, calculating the most common size that seems best to represent the majority of human bodies.

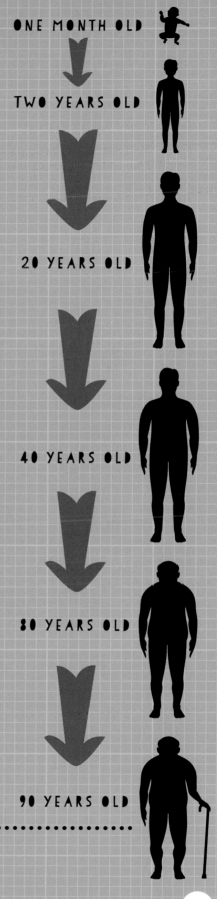

ONE MONTH OLD

TWO YEARS OLD

20 YEARS OLD

40 YEARS OLD

80 YEARS OLD

90 YEARS OLD

THERE ARE 100 TRILLION GOOD BACTERIA LIVING ON THE HUMAN BODY

Bacteria are life forms, many existing as single cells that live in the air, the ground, and in all living things, including humans.

GOOD AND BAD BACTERIA

The human body comes into contact with both good and bad bacteria every day. Good bacteria help us to digest our food, help create some of the vitamins our body needs and protect us from bad bacteria.

Bad bacteria can be the cause of many infections. Common bacterial infections are those that affect the eyes, throat or skin. Bad bacteria can also cause food poisoning, meningitis and pneumonia. Fortunately, there are more good bacteria in our bodies than bad with the good bacteria feeding off the bad bacteria.

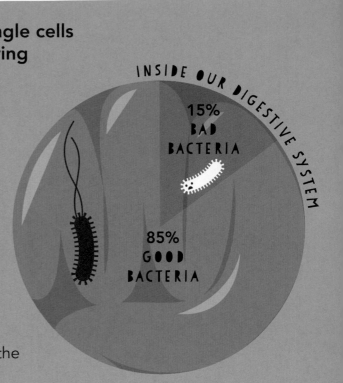

INSIDE OUR DIGESTIVE SYSTEM

15% BAD BACTERIA

85% GOOD BACTERIA

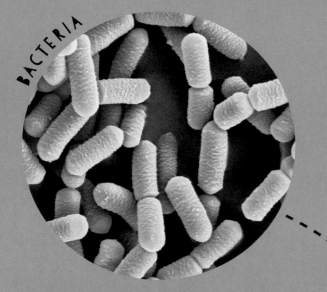

BACTERIA

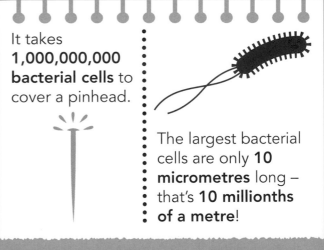

It takes **1,000,000,000 bacterial cells** to cover a pinhead.

The largest bacterial cells are only **10 micrometres** long – that's **10 millionths of a metre!**

LIVING ORGANISMS

Bacteria are a form of micro-organism – this means that they are so small, they can only be seen through a powerful microscope. Bacteria are living organisms, but are not built like animals or even the tiniest of insects; bacteria have a cell-like structure.

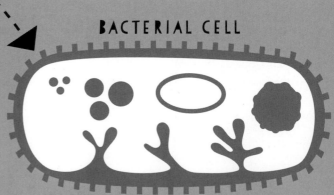

BACTERIAL CELL

BACTERIAL CELLS ARE EVERYWHERE

There are typically **40,000,000 bacterial cells** in a gram of soil.

There are about **1,000,000 bacterial cells** in a millilitre of fresh water.

Bacteria multiply in warm conditions with plenty of food and water; this includes living off the liquids and foods that pass through our bodies. **Bacteria can divide into two every 20 minutes.**

Number of minutes	Bacterial cells
20	
40	
60	
80	
100	
120	

After **six hours, one bacterium** could become **131,072 bacteria**.

There are more bacterial cells in your body than human cells. Bacterial cells outnumber human cells by a factor of **ten to one**. We are more bacteria than we are human!

WHERE?
Bacteria live all over the outside and inside of your body.

Some scientists believe that there may be **10,000,000,000,000 bacterial cells** in our digestive system, whereas others believe there could be as many as **100,000,000,000,000!** The majority of our bacteria can be found in the intestines, where they help digest our food.

THERE ARE APPROXIMATELY:
6,000,000,000 bacterial cells in your mouth. That's over **four times** the population of China.

7,000,000 bacterial cells on your arms. That's equivalent to having the population of Switzerland crawling over your arms.

3,000,000 bacterial cells on your armpits. That's the population of Mongolia in your armpits.

500,000 bacterial cells on your hands. That's the population of Luxembourg in your hands.

THERE ARE ONE TRILLION, 300 BILLION SKIN CELLS ON THE HUMAN BODY

Skin is the largest organ of the human body. It holds all our other organs together, protects our bones, muscles and internal organs, allows us to feel and react to heat and the cold. It is a huge sensor containing nerves that tell the brain what is going on around our body.

THE FUNCTIONS OF SKIN

Produces oils which act as a waterproof raincoat

Protects you from the Sun's UV rays

Keeps moisture inside the body

Regulates your body temperature

Cushions your body from strong blows

Defends your body against harmful bacteria

Skin is made up of layers of cells. There are approximately **1,300,000,000 skin cells** on the human body. Every minute you lose between **30,000 to 40,000 dead skin cells**, which are replaced by new ones. Almost all of your skin is replaced every month.

There are **two square metres of skin** covering the average human body. That's the size of a double bed sheet.

Over **50% of dust** in your home is actually dead skin.

0.05 mm thick

The thinnest area of skin on your body is on your eyelids.

The thickest area of skin is found on the soles of your feet.

1.5 mm thick

Hair

Pores

Sebaceous gland

Follicle

Blood vessels

Sweat gland

SKIN COLOUR

The colour of human skin depends on the amount of pigment, called melanin, a colouring substance that the body produces. Melanin also gives your eyes and hair their colour. The freckles on your face are also patches of melanin. Small amounts of melanin result in light skin, while large amounts result in dark skin.

SPOTS

Spots, also known as acne, are caused by an over-production of cells in the skin's sweat and sebaceous glands. Around **eight in ten** people between the ages of **11** and **30** will be affected by acne.

NAILS

Your fingernails and toenails are made of keratin which is part of the epidermis layer of skin. It is also the same substance as a bird's beak.

On average, fingernails grow **2.5 mm** in a month. Fingernails grow **four times** faster than toenails.

SKIN HAS THREE LAYERS

FIRST LAYER: EPIDERMIS

The epidermis is the top layer of skin. This layer acts as a waterproof barrier. Pores cover this layer, acting as an outlet for sweat that comes through the sweat glands. Hair also pokes through the surface.

SECOND LAYER: DERMIS

The dermis is the middle layer, where the hair and sweat glands begin.

THIRD LAYER: HYPODERMIS

The hypodermis is at the bottom, it is largely made of fatty tissue.

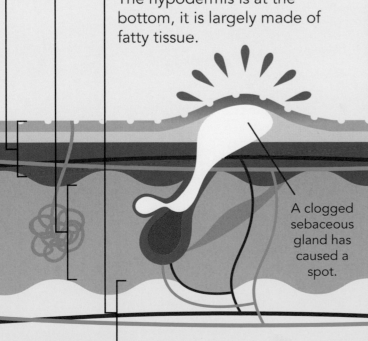

A clogged sebaceous gland has caused a spot.

Ms Lee Redmond

Ms Lee Redmond of the United States has the longest fingernails recorded in the world record books. She has been growing them for **28 years** to reach the length of **8.65 m**. That's an average growth of **30 cm** a year.

ONE YEAR: 30 CM

TEN YEARS: 3 M

TWENTY YEARS: 6 M

TWENTY-EIGHT YEARS: 8.65 M

BLONDES HAVE ONE HUNDRED AND FORTY-SIX THOUSAND STRANDS OF HAIR ON THEIR HEAD

Hair grows up from underneath the skin. It keeps you warm and helps to protect parts of your body.

HAIR FOLLICLES

Your head is covered in about **100,000 hair follicles**.

Your body is covered in about **5,000,000 hair follicles**.

Some of the hair on your body is easy to see, like your eyebrows and the hair on your head, arms and legs. But other hair, like that on your cheeks, is almost invisible. Hair can cover the whole body, with the exception of the soles of feet, palms of hands and lips.

Humans have about the same number of hair follicles as chimpanzees. Chimpanzees look hairier as their hair grows longer, thicker and darker than human hair.

HAIR GROWTH

Hair grows at around **12.7 mm per month**. It would take **10 years** to grow **1.524 m**.

One month

One year

Five years

Ten years

If a man never shaved his beard, it would grow to over nine metres in a lifetime.

9 m

HAIR LOSS

You shed around **100 hairs** on your head a day. If your hair didn't regrow, you would lose all your hair in approximately **two years and nine months**.

Eyebrow hair can last between **3–5 months** before it sheds. An eyelash can have a lifespan of about **150 days**.

Day one

Eight months, one week

One year, four months, two weeks

Two years, nine months

150

The hair that we see above the skin's surface is made of dead cells, which is why it doesn't cause any pain when someone cuts your hair.

BALDNESS

People who are bald have no hair growing on their head. The cause of baldness is believed to be genetic. This means that if your parents or grandparents or great-grandparents were bald there is an increased chance that you will also go bald. The baldness gene is much less common in women, but as women get older, their hair tends to thin out.

Some studies show that there is a four in seven chance of receiving the baldness gene.

You can begin to go bald as early as your late teens. Approximately **25%** of men begin balding by the age of **30**.

As you grow older the rate of hair regrowth slows down. **66%** of men begin balding by the age of **60**.

HAIR COLOUR

There may be an average of **100,000 strands of hair** on the human head, but the actual amount will vary depending on your hair colour.

Blondes have an average of **146,000** hair strands

People with brown hair have an average of **100,000** hair strands

Approximately **1%** of the world's population is a redhead, with **13%** of these living in Scotland.

People with black hair have an average of **110,000** hair strands

Redheads have an average of **86,000** hair strands

THE HEART BEATS ONE HUNDRED THOUSAND TIMES A DAY

The heart is one of the body's strongest muscles. It pumps blood to every part of our body making sure it receives the nutrients you need. The heart is the size of a fist and on average weighs around **300 g** – the weight of **six medium-sized eggs**.

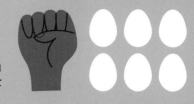

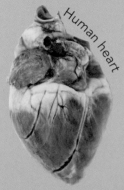
Human heart

THE HEART HAS FOUR CHAMBERS
The top two chambers are called the left atrium and right atrium. *Atrium* is Latin for 'entrance hall'.
The two lower chambers are called the left ventricle and the right ventricle. *Ventricle* is Latin for 'little belly'.
Each of the **four chambers** has a valve that makes sure the blood flows through them in **one direction**. The thumping sound of the heartbeat is the sound of the four heart valves closing.

The right side of the heart pumps blood to the lungs. The right atrium holds about **3.5 tablespoons** of blood.

The left ventricle holds just over **four tablespoons** of blood.

BLOOD CIRCULATION
The movement of blood is called circulation. The heart pumps over **7,000 l** of blood through **96,560 km** of blood vessels each day.

A newborn baby has about **one cup of blood** in circulation, but within a person's lifetime, the heart will have pumped enough blood to fill **three super tankers**.

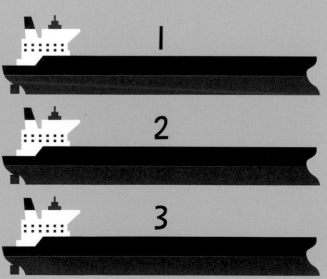

1

2

3

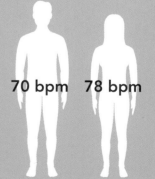

70 bpm   78 bpm

bpm = beats per minute
The heart beats to pump blood. The average heart beats **60–80 times** per minute. A woman's heart, on average, beats faster than a man's.

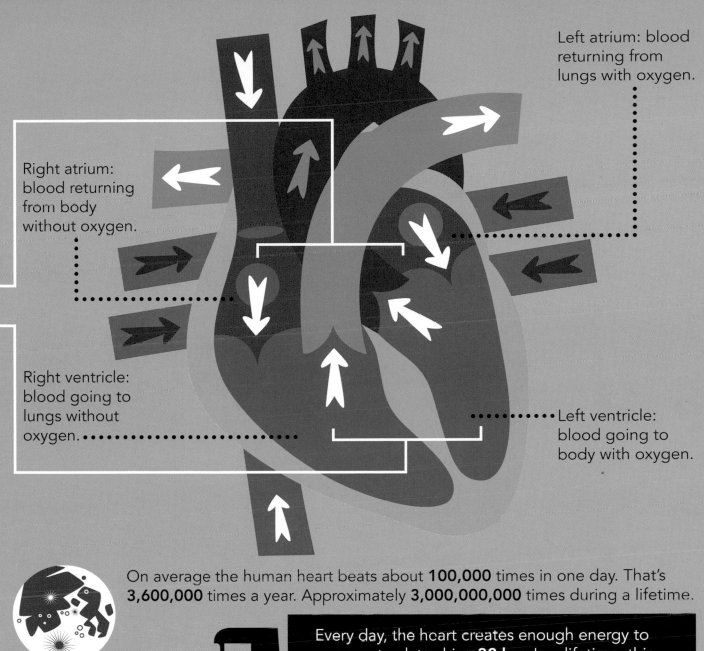

Left atrium: blood returning from lungs with oxygen.

Right atrium: blood returning from body without oxygen.

Right ventricle: blood going to lungs without oxygen.

Left ventricle: blood going to body with oxygen.

On average the human heart beats about **100,000** times in one day. That's **3,600,000** times a year. Approximately **3,000,000,000** times during a lifetime.

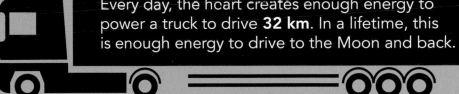

Every day, the heart creates enough energy to power a truck to drive **32 km**. In a lifetime, this is enough energy to drive to the Moon and back.

COUNTING YOUR HEARTBEAT

You can feel your heart beating and pumping blood around your body at areas called pulse points. One is on the underside of your wrist. Place two fingertips gently here to feel a beat – your pulse.

Count the number of beats for **one minute**. If you have just been exercising you will notice that the beats are faster.

Blood is a red liquid that circulates through your body. It carries oxygen and nutrients around the body and moves out waste products.
A man has approximately **5.6 l** of blood in his body.
A woman has approximately **4.5 l** of blood in her body.

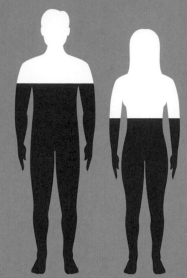

BLOOD IS MADE UP OF:

55% plasma

45% cells

Plasma is a yellow liquid in which the blood cells float. Plasma is made up of **90% water**.

THE CELLULAR COMPONENTS OF BLOOD ARE:

RED BLOOD CELLS	WHITE BLOOD CELLS	PLATELETS

1:600

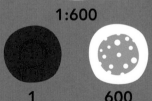

1 **600**

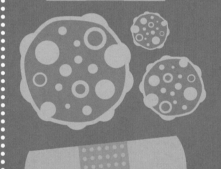

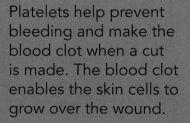

Platelets help prevent bleeding and make the blood clot when a cut is made. The blood clot enables the skin cells to grow over the wound.

A quarter of cells in the human body are red blood cells.
It takes on average **30–45 seconds** for red blood cells to circulate around the body. They are produced at a rate of **4,000,000,000 to 5,000,000,000 every hour**.

There is **one white blood cell** for every **600 red blood cells**. White blood cells are an important part of the body's immune system. They defend against certain bacteria, viruses and infectious diseases.

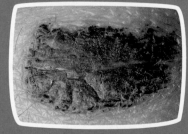

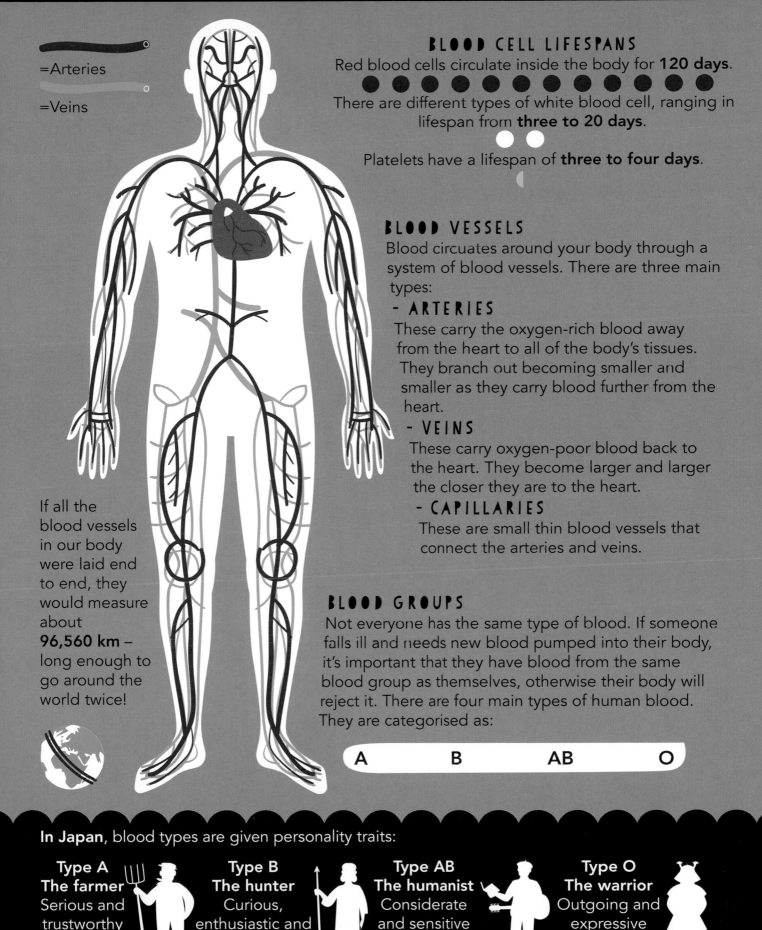

=Arteries

=Veins

BLOOD CELL LIFESPANS
Red blood cells circulate inside the body for **120 days**.

There are different types of white blood cell, ranging in lifespan from **three to 20 days**.

Platelets have a lifespan of **three to four days**.

BLOOD VESSELS
Blood circulates around your body through a system of blood vessels. There are three main types:

- **ARTERIES**
These carry the oxygen-rich blood away from the heart to all of the body's tissues. They branch out becoming smaller and smaller as they carry blood further from the heart.

- **VEINS**
These carry oxygen-poor blood back to the heart. They become larger and larger the closer they are to the heart.

- **CAPILLARIES**
These are small thin blood vessels that connect the arteries and veins.

If all the blood vessels in our body were laid end to end, they would measure about **96,560 km** – long enough to go around the world twice!

BLOOD GROUPS
Not everyone has the same type of blood. If someone falls ill and needs new blood pumped into their body, it's important that they have blood from the same blood group as themselves, otherwise their body will reject it. There are four main types of human blood. They are categorised as:

| A | B | AB | O |

In Japan, blood types are given personality traits:

Type A
The farmer
Serious and trustworthy

Type B
The hunter
Curious, enthusiastic and independent

Type AB
The humanist
Considerate and sensitive

Type O
The warrior
Outgoing and expressive

When you breathe, you breathe in oxygen and breathe out carbon dioxide.
This exchange of gases takes place in the lungs, an internal organ that forms part of the respiratory system, the system that enables you to breathe. Once in the lungs, oxygen passes through the lung walls into the red blood cells in nearby capillaries. The red blood cells then carry the oxygen around the body, generating the energy you need to live.

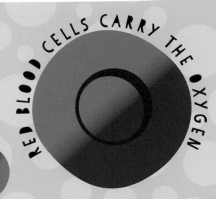

RED BLOOD CELLS CARRY THE OXYGEN

LUNGS
You have two lungs that sit in your chest. Your right lung is a little larger than your left lung as your left lung has to share its space with the heart.

HOW MANY BREATHES TO FILL?

Number of breaths

30,000,000	
28,000,000	High altitude airship: **29,449,520**
26,000,000	
24,000,000	
22,000,000	
20,000,000	
18,000,000	
16,000,000	
14,000,000	Hot air balloon: **14,724,760**
12,000,000	
10,000,000	
8,000,000	
6,000,000	
4,000,000	
2,000,000	
	Blimp: **1,147,965**
4	Party balloon: **4**
1	Lungs: **1**
0	

BREATHS

You normally breathe in **500 ml** of air with each breath. When you sleep you require less oxygen than when you are running around or playing sport. When resting, the average adult breathes around **12 to 20 times a minute**. If you were to breathe **20 times a minute**, you would have breathed in **10 l** of air.

Number of breaths:
One hour: 30
Six hours: 180
12 hours: 360
24 hours: 720

Humans breathe in between **8,000** and **9,000 l of air** each day.

When you breathe in, the air travels down through your nose or mouth, down through your throat and into your windpipe.

The windpipe splits into two smaller tubes: one goes to the left lung and the other to the right lung.

The inside of your lungs is like a giant sponge, filled with a mass of tubes. The tubes from the windpipe divide a further **15 to 25 times** into thousands of smaller airways that eventually lead to tiny air sacs, called alveoli.

ALVEOLI

An average adult's lungs can contain around **480,000,000 alveoli.**

Lungs expand and contract – like filling a balloon up with air and then deflating it.
You have muscles that help you breathe, such as your diaphragm, which sits beneath the lungs. When you breathe in, your breathing muscles contract, pulling your ribs up and out. The space within your chest increases and air flows into your lungs. When you breathe out, your muscles relax and your ribs move down and in. The space within your chest decreases and air flows out.

MORE THEN SIX HUNDRED MUSCLES IN YOUR BODY

All movement in the body is powered by your muscles.
Different sources group muscles differently and so it is difficult to state the exact number of muscles in the human body. All sources have the number of muscles above **600**; some sources have categorised as many as **850 muscles** in the body.

40% of your body weight is made up of muscle.

THERE ARE THREE TYPES OF MUSCLE

Skeletal muscles
These are muscles attached to the bones and help them move. They are areas of stretchy tissue, built up in layers.

Cardiac muscle
This is the muscle that the heart is made of.

Smooth muscle
These are found in the walls of your internal organs, such as the arteries that carry the blood around your body.

Some muscles are involuntary. They work without us thinking, like our heart beating. Other muscles are voluntary. They are controlled by our thoughts and allow us to move things around, including ourselves.

It takes **43 muscles** to frown. It takes **17 muscles** to smile.

HOW THEY WORK
Muscles work by expanding and contracting. When the biceps contract the triceps relaxes, and this allows our arm to bend. When we straighten our arm back out, the biceps will relax and the triceps will contract.

Many of our muscles come in pairs, like the biceps and triceps. Muscle pairs allow us to move parts of our body back and forth.

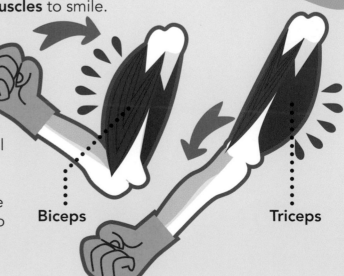

Biceps

Triceps

IMPORTANT MUSCLES AND HOW THEY HELP US

Abdominal muscles help support your body upright.

The shortest and smallest muscle is in our ears and is called the **stapedius**. It is attached to the smallest bone in the body, the stapes. At around **1.27 mm**, this muscle helps conduct sound vibrations allowing us to hear.

Pectoralis muscles help you pull and push objects.

The hardest working muscle is the **heart**, performing the largest quantity of physical work in the course of a lifetime.

Biceps and triceps help you lift up objects.

The largest muscle is the **gluteus maximus**, which makes up part of your buttocks.

The longest muscle in the human body is the **sartorius**. It runs from the hip to the knee on the inside of the leg and helps us bend the knee and twist our leg. This muscle can be as long as **60 cm**.

Quadriceps help you lift up your knee.

Calf muscles help you walk, run and jump.

EXERCISE

When we exercise, we work our muscles allowing them to become bigger and stronger, but we should not just focus on building muscles. If you have too much muscle bulk, you may find your movement restricted and find you become short of breath, putting a strain on your heart. It's important to perform aerobic exercise, such as running, which will keep your heart healthy.

RECOMMENDED LEVELS OF EXERCISE FOR ADULTS, PER WEEK:

Two hours and 30 minutes
Moderate aerobic activity, such as cycling or fast walking.
And muscle-strengthening activities on two or more days that week.
Or
One hour and 15 minutes
Intensive aerobic activity, such as running or a game of tennis.
And muscle-strengthening activities on two or more days that week.
Muscle-strengthening activities could include lifting weights, yoga or even gardening.

206 BONES IN THE HUMAN BODY

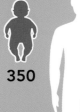

350

206

The skeleton is a framework of bones.
It holds our body up, protects vital organs and has joints attached to muscles that allow us to move.

When we are babies we have **350 bones** in our body. As we grow some bones join together and we end up with **206 bones** by the time we reach adulthood.

WHAT ARE BONES MADE OF?
Bones are made up of layers of hard tissue that have a spongy inner layer that surrounds soft tissue called bone marrow. Bone marrow is where blood cells are made, leaving the bone through tiny holes.

STRONG AND LIGHT
Bones are strong enough to support your weight, but also light enough to allow movement.

Actual size

The stape, which is inside your ear, is the smallest bone in your body measuring **3mm**.

The thigh bone, known as the femur, is the longest, largest and strongest bone in your body. The femur is **26%** of the person's height.

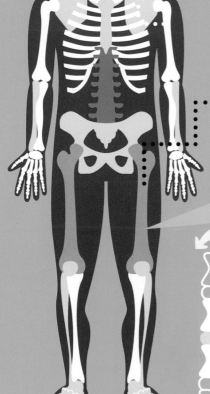

VERTEBRAL COLUMN
The vertebral column is also known as the backbone, or spine. It is a column of **24 individual bones** called vertebrae. The column extends from the base of the skull down to the bottom of the back. Each vertebrae is connected by joints, similar to a tiny ball and socket joint. The joints are surrounded by rubbery tissue called cartilage that cushions the movement of the bones.

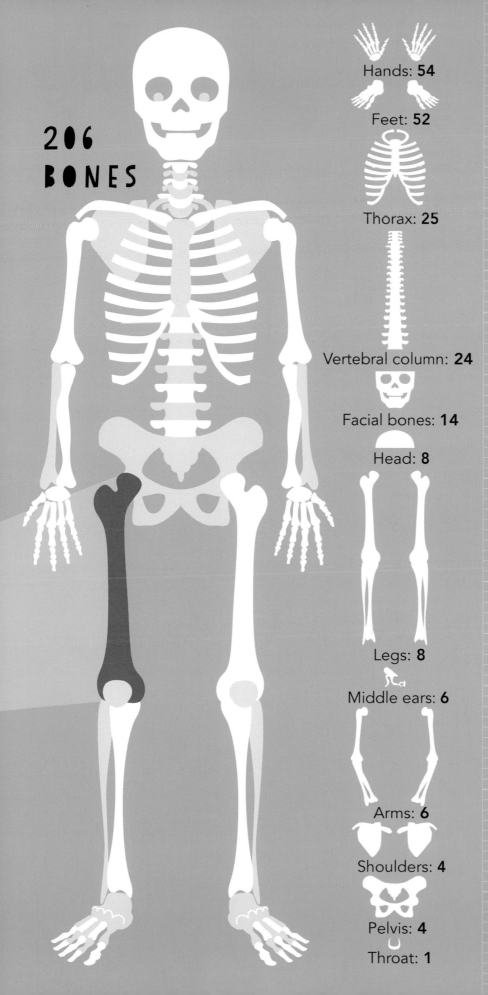

206 BONES

Hands: **54**

Feet: **52**

Thorax: **25**

Vertebral column: **24**

Facial bones: **14**

Head: **8**

Legs: **8**

Middle ears: **6**

Arms: **6**

Shoulders: **4**

Pelvis: **4**

Throat: **1**

FRACTURES

A fracture is the medical term for a broken bone. Fractures can take anything between **three to ten weeks** to heal. The younger you are the quicker they are likely to mend.

There are many different types of fracture, depending on the kind of break and injury to the bone. Here are **eight** different types:

TRANSVERSE | OBLIQUE | SPIRAL | COMMINUTED

AVULSED | IMPACTED | TORUS | GREENSTICK

TEETH

Teeth are part of the skeletal structure, but are not counted as bones as they are made from different material.

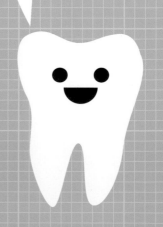

12-72 HOURS TO DIGEST FOOD

Food provides us with the fuel our body needs to grow and the energy our body needs so that we can move. When we eat food, it travels through our body in the digestive system. This system is made up of a series of organs that extract nutrients from food. The food that our body doesn't need comes out of our anus as poo.

JOURNEY TIME

Food can take anything from **12 hours** to **72 hours** to travel through the digestive system. This is largely down to the type of food you have eaten. Foods that are rich in fibre, such as fruit, will travel through the digestive system quickly, where as foods such as red meat take much longer to break down into waste matter.

SALIVA

Your mouth produces around **1 to 1.5 l** of saliva a day.

2% enzymes
98% water

Saliva is mostly water but contains a small percentage of enzymes. Enzymes are digestive juices that are good at breaking down food into tiny pieces.

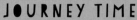

12 HOURS

72 HOURS

Food takes up to **eight seconds** to travel down the oesophagus into the stomach.

POO
The average human will produce around **163.29 kg** of poo a year.
That's just under **450 g** of poo in a day.

POO IS MADE UP OF:

- 75% water
- 8% indigestible fibres
- 8% dead bacteria
- 4% fats
- 4% salts
- 1% protein

THE STOMACH

contains acid. Along with the stomach walls, the acid breaks the food into tiny pieces. Good bacteria in the stomach attacks any harmful bacteria that may have travelled down.

THE ACID

in the stomach means that the stomach has to replace its lining every **three to four days**. That's anything between **91 to 122 stomach linings** a year.

THE LIVER

has over **500 different functions** that help our body. Within the digestive system it releases a yellowish brown fluid, called bile, that helps to break down fats within food.

THE PANCREAS

releases enzymes that break down the food into even tinier pieces and help absorb nutrients from the food.

THE SMALL INTESTINE

absorbs all the remaining nutrients from the food. These nutrients pass through the intestine's lining into your blood, which then circulates around your body. These nutrients are important for the growth of your cells.

THE LARGE INTESTINE

converts food waste into faeces, also known as poo. Poo leaves the body through the anus.

THE INTESTINES

The small intestine is around **6 m** long. It is almost **four times** as long as the average adult is tall. The large intestine is **1.5 m** long.

They are so named as the diameter of the small intestine is much smaller than that of the large intestine.

NINE MONTHS FOR A BABY TO GROW IN THE WOMB

Between the ages of eight and 15 the female body goes through a period called puberty. During this time the body goes through changes that make it possible for women to conceive and have babies.

PREGNANCY

A baby starts to grow after its mother's egg joins with its father's sperm. It takes approximately **nine months** for a baby to grow until it is ready to be born. The period of time inside the womb is called pregnancy. During the pregnancy the baby will develop all of its limbs and internal organs.

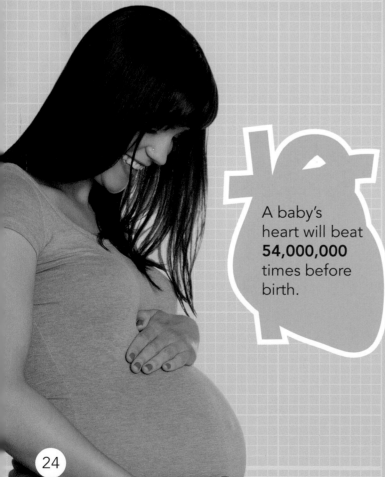

A baby's heart will beat **54,000,000** times before birth.

TAKING SHAPE

As the baby grows within the womb, its different body organs begin to take shape at different times.

Week one

Week six: arms and legs start to take shape.

Week eight: lungs, ears, eyes start to form. The developing baby is now called a foetus.

Week nine: fingers and toes are defined.

Week 14: nose, lips and taste buds are formed.

Week 25: hair has recognisable colour and texture.

Week 35-40: the baby is usually born during this period.

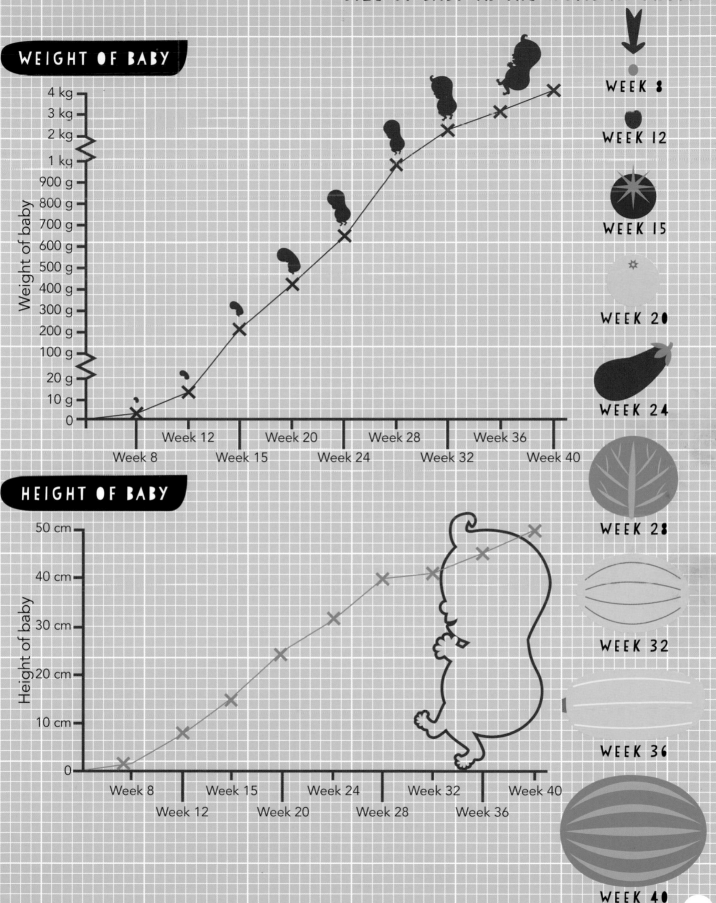

SIZE OF BABY IN THE WOMB AS FRUIT

WEEK 8
WEEK 12
WEEK 15
WEEK 20
WEEK 24
WEEK 28
WEEK 32
WEEK 36
WEEK 40

WEIGHT OF BABY

Weight of baby

4 kg
3 kg
2 kg
1 kg
900 g
800 g
700 g
600 g
500 g
400 g
300 g
200 g
100 g
20 g
10 g
0

Week 8 Week 12 Week 15 Week 20 Week 24 Week 28 Week 32 Week 36 Week 40

HEIGHT OF BABY

Height of baby

50 cm
40 cm
30 cm
20 cm
10 cm
0

Week 8 Week 12 Week 15 Week 20 Week 24 Week 28 Week 32 Week 36 Week 40

FIVE SENSES

The human body has five sense organs that gather information on the world around you.

YOUR TONGUE is covered with between **2,000** to **10,000 tiny bumps**, called taste buds. You have more taste buds the younger you are; they become weaker and die out as you get older.

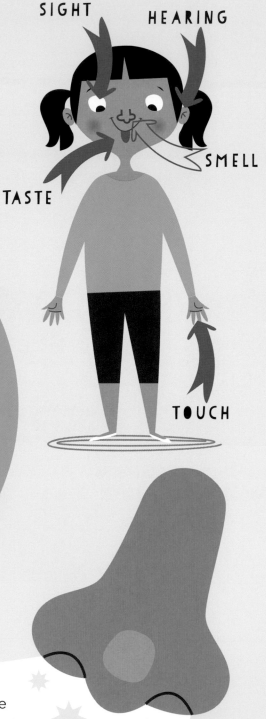

SIGHT
HEARING
SMELL
TASTE
TOUCH

YOUR TASTE BUDS DETECT FIVE MAIN TASTES:

UMAMI

SOUR

BITTER

SWEET

SALTY

The taste buds that recognise these flavours are spread over the tongue in different densities.

YOUR NOSE breathes in particles from the air and is able to pick out smells that they contain.

The average person's nose can detect more than **10,000 different smells**. When you have a blocked nose, food may have little to no taste. This is because your sense of smell works with the sense of taste to detect the flavour of food. Your sense of smell is much stronger than your sense of taste. Approximately **80%** of what we taste is understood through our sense of smell.

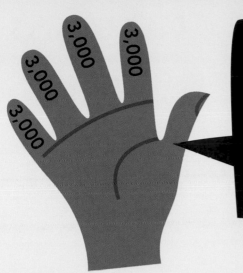

3,000 3,000 3,000 3,000 3,000

TOUCH

You have cells, called receptors, that are near the surface of your skin. These receptors are able to detect pain, pressure, touch and temperature. They are able to tell you whether an object is hard or soft, hot or cold, sharp or blunt.
There are about **3,000 touch receptors** in each of your fingers.

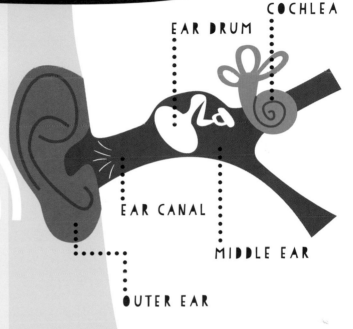

COCHLEA
EAR DRUM
EAR CANAL
MIDDLE EAR
OUTER EAR

HEARING

Sound travels through the air in sound waves. Your outer ear catches the sound waves and they travel into the ear canal. Their vibrations are felt on the ear drum and against tiny hairs. These sensations travel to the brain where the waves are translated into the sounds that we hear.
We have approximately **15,000 hair cells** in each ear.

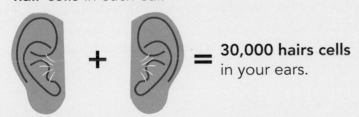

= **30,000 hairs cells** in your ears.

SIGHT

Light bounces off objects and enters your eye through the pupil. A lens in the eye focuses the light on the retina at the back of the eye ball. Light sensitive cells in the retina pick up the image, but upside down. This image is sent to your brain which turns it the right way round.

Your pupils widen and narrow to let in different amounts of light.

When it is dark, your pupils widen to let in more light so that you can see more.

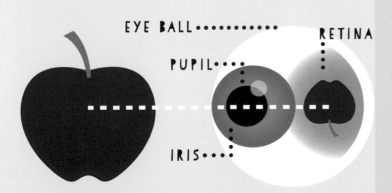

EYE BALL
RETINA
PUPIL
IRIS

THE HUMAN BRAIN WEIGHS 1.4 KILOGRAMS

Your senses send information to the brain through the nervous system. The brain translates this information into the smells, sights, sounds, tastes and physical sensations that we recognise.

THE NERVOUS SYSTEM

The brain and your spinal cord form the main components of the central nervous system. Together, they act as your body's control centre. The spinal cord is a long, thin cable of nerve fibres. It gathers together the pathways of nerves which run through your body, connecting to every organ and muscle. It is the channel for carrying messages from these nerves to and from your brain.

THE BRAIN

The brain sits inside your skull. The brain is the place where thoughts, emotions and memories are processed. It controls your movement, skills and the functions necessary to live. It is made up of over **100,000,000,000 nerve cells**. Nerve cells in the brain are also known as neurons. You could fit **30,000 neurons** on the head of a pin. You would need over **33,333,333 pinheads** to contain all of the brain's neurons.

The brain also contains over **643 km** of blood vessels. That's the same distance a car would have to drive to get from London to Edinburgh, or Washington DC to Warren, Michigan.

LONDON

EDINBURGH

28

The brain is a jelly-like mass of ridges and grooves.

78%

Approximately **78%** of your brain is water.

AVERAGE BRAIN SIZE:

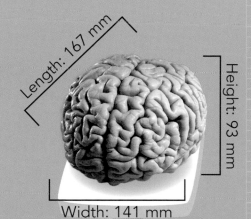

Length: 167 mm

Height: 93 mm

Width: 141 mm

Weight: 1.4 kg

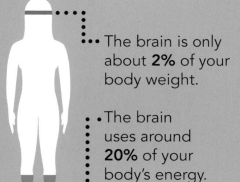

The brain is only about **2%** of your body weight.

The brain uses around **20%** of your body's energy.

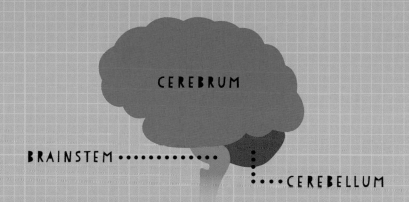

CEREBRUM

BRAINSTEM

CEREBELLUM

THE BRAIN IS MADE OF THREE MAIN PARTS

The cerebrum is the largest part of the human brain. It's the area that allows you to think, understand sensory perceptions and store memories.

The cerebellum controls your balance and tells your muscles how to move.

The brainstem connects the brain to the spinal cord. It controls the involuntary muscles that work without us thinking, such as the internal organs, including the heart, lungs and stomach.

TWO SIDES OF THE BRAIN

The cerebrum is divided down the middle into a right hemisphere and a left hemisphere. Each hemisphere appears to be specialised for some behaviours.

The right side of the brain controls muscles on the left side of the body and the left side of the brain controls muscles on the right side of the body.

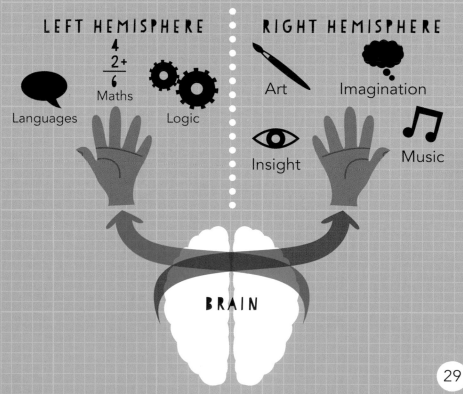

LEFT HEMISPHERE

$\frac{4}{6}$ 2+

Maths

Languages

Logic

RIGHT HEMISPHERE

Art

Imagination

Insight

Music

BRAIN

FURTHER INFORMATION

BOOKS
Essential Life Science: The Human Body by Melanie Waldron (Raintree, 2013)
Project Science: The Human Body by Sally Hewitt (Franklin Watts, 2013)
Superscience: Human Body by Rob Colson (Franklin Watts, 2013)
The World of Infographics: The Human Body by Jon Richards and Ed Simkins (Wayland, 2013)

WEBSITES
Interactive site with games and quizzes:
http://www.bbc.co.uk/science/humanbody/body/index_interactivebody.shtml
Videos, quizzes, and word searches covering all parts of the human body:
http://kidshealth.org/kid/htbw/
Short videos, text and images covering the different systems of the human body:
www.kidsbiology.com/human_biology/

Note to parents and teachers:
Every effort has been made by the publisher to ensure that these websites contain no inappropriate or offensive material. However, because of the nature of the Internet, it is impossible to guarantee that the content of these sites will not be altered. We strongly advise that Internet access is supervised by a responsible adult.

LARGE NUMBERS

1,000,000,000,000,000,000,000,000,000,000,000 = ONE DECILLION

1,000,000,000,000,000,000,000,000,000,000 = ONE NONILLION

1,000,000,000,000,000,000,000,000,000 = ONE OCTILLION

1,000,000,000,000,000,000,000,000 = ONE SEPTILLION

1,000,000,000,000,000,000,000 = ONE SEXTILLION

1,000,000,000,000,000,000 = ONE QUINTILLION

1,000,000,000,000,000 = ONE QUADRILLION

1,000,000,000,000 = ONE TRILLION

1,000,000,000 = ONE BILLION

1,000,000 = ONE MILLION

1000 = ONE THOUSAND

100 = ONE HUNDRED

10 = TEN

1 = ONE

anatomy	the scientific study of the bodily structures of humans, animals and plants
average	usual amount or an estimated or calculated means of division to find the middle number of a set
bacteria	a single-cell organism that can be found in animals, plants, earth, water and in the air
bald	an area on the body not covered with hair
carbon dioxide	a gas produced when people and animals breathe out
cell	a small element of a living organism
circulation	a movement that is circular or flows through a circuit
digestive system	a system of organs responsible for getting food in and out of your body, extracting valuable nutrients for your body's health
dissection	to cut apart in order to examine a structure
enzymes	proteins that perform chemical changes in the body
fibre	food matter that cannot be digested but helps the digestion of other food
follicle	tiny hole in the skin from where a hair grows
fracture	a crack or break in a bone
genetic	an inherited biological characteristic
glands	a group of cells or organs that combine and release substances around the body
infection	a disease caused by germs that enter the body
keratin	a protein substance that is found in hair and nails
melanin	a pigment that gives colour to skin and hair
micro-organism	organisms, like bacteria, that are too small to be seen with the naked eye
microscope	an instrument that uses lenses to magnify the image of small objects
muscles	body tissues made up of fibres that move the different parts of your body
nervous system	a system where your brain sends and receives messages through a network of nerves around your body to control movement and feeling
neurons	cells that carry messages between the brain and other parts of the body
nutrients	substances that are beneficial to growth and well-being
organism	a living thing that is able to function independently
oxygen	a gas that people and animals breathe in, necessary for life
plasma	the watery part of blood that contains blood cells
puberty	a period of growth during which a child's body develops into an adult's body, and is capable of sexual reproduction
respiratory system	the system in which the body breathes in oxygen and breathes out carbon dioxide
saliva	watery fluid that gets released in the mouth and aids digestion
tissue	a collection of cells that have a similar structure and function
umami	a taste sensation that is savoury and meaty
vessels	veins or arteries that carry blood through the body

INDEX